PITCHING HACKS!

(how to pitch startups to investors)

BY VENTURE HACKS

Formatting inspired by Edward Tufte and 37signals. Edited by Russ
Rizzo. Beta tested by many — thank you.

First edition

Thanks for buying Pitching Hacks.
Please don't make copies of this book.
You can buy it at http://venturehacks.com/pitching.
Yo!

CONTENTS

Disclaimer   7

Introduction   9

Summary   11

Traction   12

    What is traction?

    Traction speaks louder than words

Introductions   18

    Why do I need an introduction?

    Who makes the best introductions?

    Who makes the worst introductions?

    How do I get an introduction?

    What should I send middlemen?

High-Concept Pitches   29

What's a high-concept pitch?

What makes a good high-concept pitch?

Why should I write a high-concept pitch?

Aren't high-concept pitches too simple?

From incoherent to high-concept

Elevator Pitches   39

What's an elevator pitch?

Why should I craft an elevator pitch?

Dissecting the elevator pitch

Elevator pitches with bullets

Decks   50

What's a deck?

The best deck template in the universe

Tell a story with the slides

Format your deck

Business Plans   60

A sales pitch is not a business plan

NDAs   65

    Can I get investors to sign an NDA?

    Pros and cons to sending a deck

    Your deck can get in the hands of the competition

    When to send a deck

Grockit Interview   74

Pitching Resources   77

Startup Resources   79

About the Authors   82

DISCLAIMER

This book provides information, not legal advice. Use it at your own risk.

Information is not the same as legal advice. Legal advice is the formal application of information to an individual's specific circumstances.

Although we strive to make our information accurate and useful, you should consult a lawyer before applying it to your particular situation.

We do not take responsibility for rashes, financial ruin, or any other misfortune that follows — either directly or indirectly — from applying the information in this book.

We are not lawyers. Get a lawyer.

Tell me a story.

— EVERY CHILD

INTRODUCTION

Investors don't invest in businesses. They invest in stories about businesses.

If you want to raise money on favorable terms, you need multiple investment offers. How do you get multiple offers? Tell a good story to several investors at the same time. A good story can't sell a pile of garbage, but it will keep a gem from going unnoticed.

You can tell a story in a sentence; you can tell a story in a paragraph; and you can tell a story in a 20-minute pitch. Startups need to do all three.

We've founded companies like Epinions; helped start companies that are backed by Sequoia, Benchmark, and Kleiner Perkins; raised $100M or so for startups; and invested another $20M in about 12 companies. This book summarizes some of the lessons we've learned about pitching companies to investors.

With modifications, you can also use these techniques to pitch prospective employees, partners, customers, and anyone else you seek to influence.

Many successful investors and entrepreneurs, such as Marc Andreessen, David Cowan, and Brad Feld, have generously contributed passages sprinkled throughout this weighty tome.

Many of the ideas in this book first appeared on venturehacks.com — that was our first draft. With the feedback of our readers and beta testers, we have created this book — a second draft. Please enjoy, and send us feedback — so the next revision is even better. We can't respond to every e-mail, but we do read and appreciate them all. *Thank you!*

NIVI AND NAVAL
team@venturehacks.com

San Francisco, California
January 2009

SUMMARY

Pitching Hacks, in one page.

Don't spam investors with your business plan. Instead, convince **middlemen** to introduce you to investors. An effective middleman is simply someone investors listen to — often another entrepreneur or investor.

Find middlemen by picking up the phone and calling everyone you know, who knows investors well, who will listen to you. Then use these tools to pitch middlemen and investors alike:

1. An **elevator pitch**. The major components of an elevator pitch are traction, product, team, and social proof. And investors care about traction over everything else.

2. Your elevator pitch should include a **high-concept pitch**: a single sentence that distills your startup's vision. A high-concept pitch is the perfect meme for fans and investors who are spreading the word about your company.

3. Also consider sending investors a "ten-slide" **deck** that tells a compelling story about your team, product, traction, and plans.

4. You don't need a "**business plan**."

Finally, don't ask for an **NDA** — investors won't sign one. Your elevator pitch and deck probably won't get in the hands of the competition, but you should assume they will. So don't share information that must remain confidential.

Chapter 1

TRACTION

Traction is a measure of your product's engagement with its market. Investors care about traction over everything else.

What is traction?

Traction speaks louder than words

For investors, the product is nothing.

— Marc Hedlund
Founder, Wesabe

What is traction?

Whether they're reading an elevator pitch or listening to a presentation, investors care most about *actual* traction in a *seemingly* large market.

Traction is a measure of your product's engagement with its market, *a.k.a.* product/market fit. In order of importance, it is demonstrated through profit, revenue, customers, pilot customers, non-paying users, and verified hypotheses about customer problems. And their rates of change.

A story without traction is a work of fiction. You must start building your product and start testing it with your market before you start raising money.

If this seems impossible, reduce scope. Put your idea on a piece of paper and start testing it with customers: "Does this solve your problem? How much would you pay for it?" This is the kind of data that can sway investors, even if your product is only a piece of paper.

Investors want to invest in startups that will be successful with or without them. And those who succeed don't wait for investors before they begin to create. They can't wait to carry their idea forward.

Traction speaks louder than words

If you have incredible traction in what seems to be a large market, you can raise money no matter what the product and team look like — although a good product and team will improve your terms.

If you have some traction and the market seems large, your product and team are both critical to raising money.

If you have *no* traction, a great demo or a previously successful team are essential.

And if the market doesn't seem large, investors won't care about your product, team, or company at all.

In general, the more you need money, the less likely that you're going to get it. But making something out of nothing is what entrepreneurs do.

In a great market – a market with lots of real potential customers – the market pulls product out of the startup. The market needs to be fulfilled and the market will be fulfilled, by the first viable product that comes along.

The product doesn't need to be great; it just has to basically work. And, the market doesn't care how good the team is, as long as the team can produce that viable product. In short, customers are knocking down your door to get the product; the main goal is to actually answer the phone and respond to all the e-mails from people who want to buy.

And when you have a great market, the team is remarkably easy to upgrade on the fly. This is the story of search keyword advertising, and Internet auctions, and TCP/IP routers.

Conversely, in a terrible market, you can have the best product in the world and an absolutely killer team, and it doesn't matter – you're going to fail. You'll break your pick for years trying to find customers who don't exist for your marvelous product, and your wonderful team will eventually get demoralized and quit, and your startup will die. This is the story of videoconferencing, and workflow software, and micropayments... ☞

...Whenever you see a successful startup, you see one that has reached product/market fit – and usually along the way screwed up all kinds of other things, from channel model to pipeline development strategy to marketing plan to press relations to compensation policies to the CEO sleeping with the venture capitalist. And the startup is still successful.

Do whatever is required to get to product/market fit. Including changing out people, rewriting your product, moving into a different market, telling customers no when you don't want to, telling customers yes when you don't want to, raising that fourth round of highly dilutive venture capital – whatever is required.

> — *Marc Andreessen, Founder, Netscape*
> "The Pmarca Guide to Startups, part 4:
> The only thing that matters"
> *blog.pmarca.com*

Chapter 2
INTRODUCTIONS

Don't spam investors with your business plan. Instead, convince middlemen to introduce you to investors. An effective middleman is simply someone investors listen to. Find middlemen by picking up the phone and calling everyone you know, who knows investors well, who will listen to you.

Why do I need an introduction?

How do I get an introduction?

Who makes the best introductions?

Who makes the worst introductions?

What should I send middlemen?

VCs are generally bombarded by requests for meetings, so a warm introduction helps an entrepreneur's request float to the top of the list.

— CHRIS WAND
Foundry Group, Investors in
Zynga

Why do I need an introduction?

You're not the only entrepreneur in the world who is trying to raise money. Investors get more requests for meetings than they can accommodate in this lifetime or the next. So they use introductions to prioritize and filter meeting requests.

You *could* send investors a cold e-mail, but your traction, team, or product better be mind-blowing — and they probably aren't.

Getting an introduction is a test of your entrepreneurial skills. If you can't convince a middleman to make an introduction, how will you convince employees to join your company? How will you convince customers to buy from you? How will you convince investors to put their money in your pocket?

Who makes the best introductions?

An effective middleman is simply someone investors listen to.

But not all middlemen are created equal. The quality of the middleman helps investors prioritize meeting requests. It's easier to land a meeting with a high-quality middleman. And if the middleman sucks, you won't get a meeting.

Who makes the best introductions? In rough order of effectiveness:

1. Entrepreneurs whom the investor has backed and made money with, wants to back, or is currently backing.

2. Other investors whom the investor has co-invested and made money with, wants to co-invest with, or is currently co-investing with.

3. Market, product, and technology experts such as senior executives at dominant companies or lauded professors.

4. Lawyers, accountants, and sundry industry people like us.

5. Communists.

6. Someone the investor met at a party once.

Use this list to measure a middleman's potential. But the details of a middleman's relationship with investors are more important than this list. So ask your middleman questions like:

> "How do you know the investor? What have you done together? What companies have you sent him that he has subsequently backed? What makes our company interesting enough for you to make an introduction?"

Who makes the worst introductions?

There are some introductions that hurt more than they help.

First, investors who decline to invest in your company may offer to introduce you to other investors. An introduction by an investor who makes it a habit to invest in businesses like yours, but doesn't want to invest, is a useless introduction. So skip these introductions if the first investor doesn't have a good reason to not invest.

Instead, ask the first investor who he wants to introduce you to. Then get your own introductions to these investors.

Second, you don't want introductions from middlemen who investors barely know. Or middlemen who investors don't trust. These introductions just make you look bad. Use the questions in the previous section to weed out these middlemen. If an introduction starts with "I don't know if you remember me," you're in trouble.

How do I get an introduction?

Pick up the phone and call everyone you know, who knows investors well, and will listen to you. Call in all your favors to get the attention of middlemen.

Explain why investors will appreciate the introduction. How? Use the high-concept pitch and elevator pitch that we describe in the following chapters.

If you're building an interesting company, people will offer to introduce you to investors. It makes them looks good. In Hollywood, *content is king*. In Silicon Valley, *dealflow is king*.

Get the middleman to focus on making a single great introduction. Three weak e-mail introductions won't do anything, but one strong phone call might.

If you're having no luck convincing middlemen to make introductions, consider making them advisors as an incentive or reward.

If that doesn't work, ask the middleman to recommend investors or other middlemen:

"Can you suggest just one person we should be talking to? We'll find our own way to him or her, and we won't use your name."

If you can't find middlemen who know investors at all, start asking people "Who do you know, who knows investors?"

Finally, if you can't get a single introduction to an investor who makes it a habit to invest in companies like yours, go back to the drawing board. Grow your company to the point where investors get interested. Go work at a startup and make the right connections. Hang out in the lobby of conferences and make the right connections. Start blogging about your company. Sit down with your team and brainstorm about how to get introductions. Brainstorm about how to get your company to a point where you can get an introduction. [1]

Nobody said this was fast or easy.

---

[1] See Marc Andreessen's "When the VCs say 'no'" for more advice: tinyurl.com/yutrb8

What should I send middlemen?

Send an elevator pitch that the middleman can forward to investors with a thumbs-up. Also consider attaching a deck. Don't ask for an NDA from the investor or the middleman. Don't send a business plan or executive summary.

We'll cover all of these topics in the following chapters.

Follow the introductions. Your lead investor will likely be a friend of an angel who you met through the advisor you met at your girlfriend's father's 55th birthday party.

We spoke with 16 angels and 12 VCs. Angels made 24 introductions; VCs only made four. The average angel introduced us to 1.5 other investors, but the average VC only introduced us to 0.33 other investors. That's a 5x difference!

> — *Adam Smith, Founder, Xobni*
> "Raising Money, Some Data and Tactical Advice, Letters to Graduating YC Companies, Letter 2"
> *xobni.com*

In my environment – a middle sized Midwestern city (Fort Wayne, IN), the middleman list is a bit broader (and we are typically talking to angels, not VCs). It would include economic development people, business incubator people (that's what I do for a living at the moment – a tech incubator, see niic.net), local government officials (city council, county council, state representatives), and the local business press. In my setting they'd probably rank somewhere between 2 and 3 on your list.

> — *Steve Franks*
> Personal communication
> *niic.net*

At Industrial Interface, we have come across "pay for introduction" types of middlemen. We've worked with a couple of the groups, and had varying levels of success. We are currently working with a professional middlemen group that charges us, but has had valuable advice – they've changed my opinion of the pay-to-play introduction scene. For a group like ours, with few industry connections, using a professional (who also usually offers consulting advice on business documents) is a necessity. However, in my experience, most of them are not worth the money.

> — *Travis Leleu*
> Personal communication
> *industrialinterface.com*

Chapter 3

HIGH-CONCEPT PITCHES

Distill your company's vision into a single phrase or sentence. A high-concept pitch is the perfect meme for fans and investors who are spreading the word about your company.

What's a high-concept pitch?

What makes a good high-concept pitch?

Why should I write a high-concept pitch?

Aren't high-concept pitches too simple?

From incoherent to high-concept

Summarize the company's business on the back of a business card.

— SEQUOIA CAPITAL
Investors in Google

What's a high-concept pitch?

A high-concept pitch distills a startup's vision into a single phrase or sentence.

Hollywood has perfected the art of the high-concept pitch:

"It's Jaws in space!" *(Alien)*

"A serial killer who bases murders on the seven deadly sins!" *(Se7en)*

"A bus with a bomb!" *(Guess.)*

"Snakes on a plane!" *(Do we really have to spell it out for you?)*

"Bambi meets Terminator!" *(Okay, we made this one up.)*

Every startup should also have a high-concept pitch:

"Friendster for dogs." *(Dogster)*

"Flickr for video." *(YouTube)*

"We network networks." *(Cisco)*

"The Firefox of media players." *(Songbird)*

"Massively Multiplayer Online Learning." *(Grockit)*

"The entrepreneurs behind the entrepreneurs." *(Sequoia Capital)*

"Create your own social network." *(Ning)*

"Venture Hacks." *(Guess who.)*

What makes a good high-concept pitch?

First, the pitch should be brief. One short sentence or phrase is perfect.

Second, your audience should already understand the building blocks of the pitch: buses, bombs, Jaws, space, the seven deadly sins, Flickr, Firefox, MMOGs, etc.

A high-concept pitch combines these building blocks to create a simple, memorable image of your startup, often by juxtaposing or drawing analogies to familiar terms; e.g. "Jaws in space." Relating your company to another well-known company is another commmon approach, e.g. "The Firefox of media players."

Third, the pitch probably isn't your company's tagline. The pitch and tagline speak to different audiences. For example, YouTube's tagline, "Broadcast Yourself," speaks to their users. Their pitch, "Flickr for video," speaks to potential investors, employees, and the press.

Finally, you may be able to develop a pitch that's also a tagline. Cisco's "We network networks" speaks to their customers *and* investors. But separate pitches and taglines are just fine.

Why should I write a high-concept pitch?

First, your fans need a simple way to spread the word about your business. Investors use the high-concept pitch when they describe your startup to other investors. Customers use the pitch when they rave about your product. And the press uses it when they cover your company. For example, see "Comparing The Flickrs of Video" on techcrunch.com.

Second, a high-concept pitch is the best way to describe your product and vision within an elevator pitch (see the next chapter). Bad elevator pitches go on and on about the product. Good ones boil it down to a high-concept pitch. The rest of the elevator pitch should be devoted to your traction, product, team, and social proof.

Aren't high-concept pitches too simple?

Some people think high-concept pitches are too simple. We agree. They are too simple — that's the point. They're the beginning of a conversation, not the end of one.

There are too many startups vying for too little attention from customers and investors. You simply won't have the opportunity to tell your whole story at once. Use a high-concept pitch to capture some attention, so you have the chance to tell the rest of your story.

How is anybody going to tell anybody about your product if you can't describe it in a few words?

From incoherent to high-concept

Anthony Stevens, an entrepreneur, read one of our blog posts on high-concept pitches and decided to write one:

> "So, let's see: my startup is Crowdify, a tool for brand and reputation managers to discover new insights into consumers' attitudes about their subjects and make better decisions about marketing and public relations strategy. We do this through semantic analysis applied to consumer-generated correlations among and between brands and reference data. Further, we utilize social-networking metaphors to keep interesting information flowing back and forth between branding people and the consuming public."

> *(From thepursuitofalife.com)*

Most elevator pitches look like this — long, boring, senseless and ineffective. You probably stopped reading after the first sentence. Or the pitch looked so long you didn't read it at all.

Fortunately, Anthony came to same conclusion:

> "That's a little wordy, especially for a business card, so let's try a little high-concept pitch development.

Hmm… relations that people will understand. "A for B", where A is a known brand in my space, and B is the target audience… how about:

'Facebook for Brands'

"I think I like it! Not least of which is the rumor floating around today that Facebook is about to be acquired by Microsoft for something like 15 to 20 billion dollars."

We like it too. Anthony started with a long paragraph that hurt him more than it helped. Then he created a high-concept pitch that opens the door to a conversation about his company.

What's your favorite high-concept pitch?

The idea is that simple concepts make for easy-to-sell movies. One corollary to that notion, of course, is that studio executives are too busy and/or too stupid to take the time to listen to a complicated pitch about a film with a multi-layered plot and nuanced characters.

> — *Karl Heitmueller, Author*
> "Sometimes 'High-Concept' Is Just Plain Old Awful"
> *toughguygoods.com*

Chapter 4

ELEVATOR PITCHES

An introduction captures an investor's attention, but a great elevator pitch gets a meeting. The major components of the elevator pitch are traction, product, team, and social proof.

What's an elevator pitch?

Why should I craft an elevator pitch?

Dissecting the elevator pitch

Elevator pitches with bullets

The elevator pitch forms everyone's first impression of your venture. It needn't be a single sentence, but the delivery ought to be measured in seconds, not minutes — like any good TV or radio commercial.

I know it sounds a little crazy, but I've come to believe that a clear, compelling elevator pitch is essential to growing a business. And I've paid dearly for the evidence.

— DAVID COWAN
Bessemer, Investors in Skype

What's an elevator pitch?

An elevator pitch is a brief e-mail that a middleman can forward with a thumbs-up. We crafted this elevator pitch using information we gleaned from one of Marc Andreessen's blog posts about Ning (Marc is also the founder of Netscape):

```
Subject: Introducing Ning to Blue Shirt
Capital

Hi [Middleman],

Thanks for offering to introduce us to
Blue Shirt Capital. I've attached a short
presentation about our company, Ning.

Briefly, Ning lets you create your own
social network for anything. For free. In
2 minutes. It's as easy as starting a
blog. Try it at: http://ning.com

We built Ning to unlock the great ideas
from people all over the world who want to
use this amazing medium in their lives.

We have over 115,000 user-created
networks, and our page views are growing
10% per week. We previously raised $44M
from Legg Mason and others, including
myself.
```

```
Before Ning, I started Netscape (acquired
by AOL for $4.2B) and Opsware (acquired by
HP for $1.6B).

Blue Shirt's investments in companies like
Extensive Enterprises tell me that they
could be a great partner for Ning. We're
starting meetings with investors next
week, and I would love to show Blue Shirt
what we're building at Ning.

Best,

Marc Andreessen
xyz@ning.com
415.555.1212
```

Your e-mail should be no longer than this example (which is already too long).

Why should I craft an elevator pitch?

Your middleman sells investors on reading your elevator pitch. The elevator pitch sells investors on reading your deck. And the deck sells investors on taking a meeting.

Many investors will just skim the deck and take a meeting if the introduction and elevator pitch are good.

Finally, if you don't have an introduction, an elevator pitch is critical to a successful cold e-mail.

Dissecting the elevator pitch

Let's dissect the elevator pitch we crafted from Marc's blog:

Subject: Introducing Ning to Blue Shirt
Capital **[A useful subject line!]**

Hi [Middleman],

Thanks for offering to introduce us to
Blue Shirt Capital. **[Reiterating the
social proof of the introducer.]** I've
attached a short presentation about our
company, Ning. **[I attached a deck.]**

Briefly, Ning lets you create your own
social network for anything. For free. In
2 minutes. **[What's the high concept pitch?
What does the product help the customer
do? Who is the customer?]** It's as easy as
starting a blog. **[What's the metaphor?]**
Try it at: http://ning.com **[Link to the
product, screencast, or screenshots.]**

We built Ning to unlock the great ideas
from people all over the world who want to
use this amazing medium in their lives.
[What's the big problem or opportunity?]

We have over 115,000 user-created networks, and our page views are growing 10% per week. [**Traction.**] We previously raised $44M from Legg Mason and others, including myself. [**More traction and social proof.**]

Before Ning, I started Netscape (acquired by AOL for $4.2B) and Opsware (acquired by HP for $1.6B). [**Team's past successes.**]

Blue Shirt's investments in companies like Extensive Enterprises tell me that they could be a great partner for Ning. [**Why are you interested in this investor?**] We're starting meetings with investors next week, and I would love to show Blue Shirt what we're building at Ning. [**Call to action and subtle scarcity.**]

Best,

Marc Andreessen
xyz@ning.com
415.555.1212 [**Contact information — how thoughtful.**]

[**OVERALL, TEH E-MAIL USEZ GOOD GRAMMER; PUNCTUASHUN, AN CAPITALIZASHUN, AS WELL AS SHORT PARAGRAFS AN SENTENCEZ.**]

When in doubt, follow this template *exactly*. It doesn't matter if you don't have Marc's successes, just explain the success you have. And keep the product description brief — this pitch describes the product in one paragraph with 29 words. The rest of the pitch should be devoted to your traction, team, and social proof.

Elevator pitches with bullets

If you're having trouble writing an elevator pitch, try using bullets.

We once received a cold e-mail that was particularly effective. It was short (88 words, not including the signature), the company demonstrated that it had good traction, and the author used bullets to make his case (four out of five bullets were about traction). Here it is, with the author's permission and identifying information redacted:

```
Subject: Cold emai [sic]

Hi

A quick "cold e-mail" to see if you would
be interested in helping [company name
redacted] raise money.

Our Story

* We are the the Facebook of [redacted]

* Over 1.5 Million registered users

* Growing at 10,000-15,000 new users per
day
```

```
* Projecting growth at 50K-60K new users
per day in next 60 days

* Zero cost per customer acquisition

If you are interested please contact me :)

Thanks
```

The prose, spelling, and formatting could use work. But the pitch was brief and effective, so we followed up with him.

Here's another example, a rewrite of Ning's elevator pitch using bullets:

```
Subject: Introducing Ning to Blue Shirt
Capital

Hi [Middleman],

Thanks for offering to introduce us to
Blue Shirt Capital. I've attached a short
presentation about Ning. Here are some of
the highlights:

* Ning lets you create your own social
network for anything. For free. In 2
minutes. It's as easy as starting a blog.
Try it at http://ning.com

* We have over 115,000 user-created
networks and our page views are growing
10% per week.

* We previously raised $44M from Legg
Mason and others, including myself.
```

* Before Ning, I started Netscape
(acquired by AOL for $4.2B) and Opsware
(acquired by HP for $1.6B).

We're building Ning to unlock the great
ideas from people all over the world who
want to use this amazing medium in their
lives.

Blue Shirt's investments in companies like
Extensive Enterprises tell me that they
could be a great partner for Ning. We're
starting meetings with investors next week
and I would love to show Blue Shirt what
we're building at Ning.

Best,

Marc Andreessen
xyz@ning.com
415.555.1212

Not bad. But at 163 words (not including the signature), it's almost twice the size of the cold call we received. Challenge yourself to keep the pitch under 100 words.

When Jim Bidzos first explained to me Ron Rivest's idea for selling public key certificates (Rivest is the R in RSA), it took a while for the math to sink in. But as I came to understand how public key cryptography facilitates encryption, authentication and (theoretically) non-repudiation, I reveled in the cleverness. Like so many spectators of greatness, I congratulated myself for comprehending this wonderful meme. So when Jim and I launched Digital Certificates, Inc. (later renamed Verisign), I proudly (and thoroughly) explained public key crypto to whomever I was recruiting as a partner, employee or co-investor. "You see, people encrypt messages today using a numeric key that they must first share with each other...blah blah... Now using one-way functions like multiplication of large prime numbers...blah blah... So if the public key decrypts the message, then that must mean...blah blah..." Surely the brilliance of the idea must compel them!

Compel? More like confuse, bore and repel. I don't think anyone (including me) really understood what our little startup needed to do until we hired our CEO Stratton Sclavos. Stratton dispensed with the math, as well as the notion that people feel the need to buy obscenely large integers with incomprehensible mathematical properties. Instead, Stratton announced that we are bringing Trust to cyberspace, and our first product is a Driver's License for the Internet. (One of these Driver's Licenses evolved into SSL certificates.)

Stratton's simple message focused on the market problem, not the underlying technology. Rather than make the audience feel stupid, Stratton crafted a metaphor that anyone can understand on even a short elevator ride.

> — *David Cowan, Partner, Bessemer*
> "Practicing the Art of Pitchcraft"
> *whohastimeforthis.com*

Chapter 5

DECKS

An introduction and elevator pitch are critical to getting a meeting. Also consider providing a "ten-slide" deck that tells a compelling story about your team, product, traction, and plans.

What's a deck?

The best deck template in the universe

Tell a story with the slides

Format your deck

PowerPoint plans greatly increase your chance of getting a term sheet, or at least the dignity of a quick no.

— DAVID COWAN
Bessemer, Investors in Staples

What's a deck?

A deck is a PowerPoint presentation that provides more details about your business. It includes sections — like problem, solution, sales, and marketing — that aren't in your elevator pitch.

A deck is less important than an elevator pitch. And an elevator pitch is less important than your middleman. Many investors will just skim a deck and take a meeting if the introduction and elevator pitch are good.

But you should still consider sending a deck with your elevator pitch. A deck lets investors learn more about your company. It demonstrates that you've thought about the company in detail. It's an industry norm. And you need one for presentations anyway.

The best deck template in the universe

Our favorite deck template comes from David Cowan at Bessemer Venture Partners. You can find other templates, but this is the best.

Here's our adaptation of David's template:

1. **Cover**. Include your logo, tagline, and complete contact information.

2. **Summary**. Summarize the key, compelling facts of the company. Make sure you cover all the topics that are in your elevator pitch — in fact, just steal the content from the elevator pitch.

3. **Team**. Highlight the past accomplishments of the team. If your team has been successful before, investors may believe it can be successful again. Include directors or advisors who bring something special to the company. Don't include positions you intend to fill — save that for the milestones slide. Put yourself last: it seems humble and lets you tell a story about how your career has led to the discovery of the...

4. **Problem**. Describe the customer, market, and problem you address, without getting into your product. Emphasize the pain level and the inability of competitors to satisfy the need.

5. **Solution**. Introduce your product and its benefits and describe how it addresses the problem you just described. Include a demo such as a screencast, a link to working software, or pictures. *God help you if you have nothing to show.*

6. **Technology**. Describe the technology behind your solution. Focus on how the technology enables the differentiated aspects of your solution. If appropriate, mention patent status.

7. **Marketing**. Who are the customers? How big is the market? You summarized this in your Problem slide and this is your opportunity to elaborate. How are you going to acquire customers? What customers have you already acquired?

8. **Sales**. What's your business model? If you have sales, discuss the sales you've made and your pipeline. What are the microeconomics and macroeconomics that turn your business into a $X million revenue business? Emphasize the microeconomics (each user is worth $1/year because...) instead of the macroeconomics (if we can get 1% of a $10B market...).

9. **Competition**. Describe why customers use your product instead of the competition's. Describe any competitive advantages that remain after the competition decides to copy you exactly. Never deny that you have competitors — it's okay to compete. Against anyone.

10. **Milestones**. Describe your current status and prospective milestones for the next 1-3 quarters for your product, team, marketing, and sales. Use a table with the quarters on the x-axis and the functions on the y-axis. Also include quarterly and cumulative gross burn (your expenses, assuming zero revenue) for the next 1-3 quarters. Don't build a detailed financial model if you don't have past earnings, a significant financial history, or insight into the issue. What hypotheses did you test in the last round of financing and what were the results? What hypotheses will you test with this round?

11. **Conclusion**. This slide can be inspirational, a larger vision of what the company could accomplish if these current plans are realized, or a rehash of the Summary slide.

12. **Financing**. Dates, amounts, and sources of money raised. How much money are you raising in this round? Restate the hypotheses that you will you test in this round.

Tell a story with the slides

This sequence of slides tells a story:

> We have a mission and a team that is taking us there. Why? We discovered this large problem and solved it with a product that has this amazing technology inside. We're going to market and sell it to these customers, with these advantages over our competitors. In particular, we're working towards these milestones over the next few quarters. In conclusion, this financing is a great investment opportunity.

This is a good sequence for a written deck. But don't take this sequence too literally when you're presenting.

You should almost always do a demo at the start of a presentation, right after you introduce yourself — even if you think the audience has already seen the demo. You can tell the audience about the rest of your team later.

Then, sequence the slides to tell a good story. Some people like to put the team slide after the technology slide. There's room to move content between the problem, marketing, and sales slides. Just make sure you cover each of the topics in the template.

Storytelling is an art, not a science — which is a nice way of saying the authors don't know the science of storytelling. But see Jason Calacanis' excellent "How To Demo Your Startup" for ideas on pitching in person: http://bit.ly/Uw4h and http://bit.ly/hUTy.

Format your deck

Keep the slides simple, visual, and minimal. Use 30 point or larger font. The slides will look great when you present.

Put talking points, reasoning, and prose in the notes that accompany each slide. Don't try to cram cogent arguments into bullet points on the slides.

E-mail investors a PDF that combines each slide and its notes on a single page — slide on top, notes on bottom. Don't e-mail a PowerPoint file unless your deck contains critical animations or movies.

You now have a single deck that you can send via e-mail or present in person. An investor can read the slides and notes together and imagine a presentation. And you can present the slides while you refer to the notes.

Finally, try Keynote if you're on a Mac. It makes beautiful decks and it's fun to use.

Obey the 10/20/30 Rule of PowerPoint. It's quite simple: a PowerPoint presentation should have ten slides, last no more than twenty minutes, and contain no font smaller than thirty points.

— *Guy Kawasaki, Managing Director, Garage*
"The 10/20/30 Rule of PowerPoint"
guykawasaki.com

The classic engineer's VC pitch has ten slides about the product and two about the academic achievements of the founders. That's a terrible pitch. One slide should be about the product, while the rest cover the market, competitors, financials, funding history, and the relevant experience of the team. The product matters far less to most investors than the reactions of customers, the properties of the market, and the credibility of the team. Obsess about the product on your own time; present your business in all of its parts.

— *Marc Hedlund, Founder, Wesabe*
"Entrepreneurial Proverbs"
radar.oreilly.com

Chapter 6

BUSINESS PLANS

Don't send long business plans to investors.

A sales pitch is not a business plan

The best way to get our attention is not with a 100-page business plan.

— CHARLES RIVER VENTURES
Investors in Twitter

A sales pitch is not a business plan

Business plans. Nobody reads them and nobody executes them. Investors who want a long plan look bad — so do companies that generate them.

The Milestones slide of your deck summarizes your company's plan for the next 1-3 quarters. Document your detailed plans on a napkin, wiki, spreadsheet, deck, to-do list, wherever. Share it with investors sometime around your second meeting and make sure they generally agree with your plan — especially your plans for testing and revise your hypotheses.

But don't send investors a 50-page sales pitch that you call a business plan — an elevator pitch and deck are sufficient. You don't need an executive summary either — an elevator pitch and deck are sufficient.

It's always a good idea to put down on paper your plans for the business, so that your team can build consensus around objectives and metrics. Make it as thick and wordy as you like (though show some restraint – over-modeling the future only wastes your time). But my advice is to never send a document like that to a VC.

Keep in mind that you are not alone – entrepreneurship is thriving around the world. In fact, we assess about 100 times as many investment opportunities as we fund, so as everyone knows, it's hard to get a VC's attention. It's not exactly true that all VC's are stupid (not exactly), but we do not have the luxury of an attention span. Drop a thick document on a VC and it will, wrapped in good intentions, go straight to The Pile.

The Pile is a dark, evil tower – impervious to attack – that looms over every VC's desk. My Pile, like many, is constructed out of business plans, white papers, analyst reports and scientific journals, waiting to be read with quiet thought and deliberation. Who Has Time For This? ☞

That's why nothing slows down a VC as much as a comprehensive business plan. PowerPoint presentations, in contrast, can be quickly e-mailed and skimmed, eliciting much faster indications of whether there is a fit. And if there is a fit, the VC will have an easier time educating the firm about the opportunity. So PowerPoint plans greatly increase your chance of getting a term sheet, or at least the dignity of a quick No.

I was first exposed to this notion in 1995 by a super smart CEO, whose name I regretfully forget. His company (Eo Networks, I think) developed fiber termination units optimized for rural networks. He was walking me through his slides, and when I asked him for his business plan, he pointed to the laptop, looked me in the eye, and said, "this is my business plan." I thought, What? Oh. Okay.

> — *David Cowan, Partner, Bessemer*
> "How To NOT Write A Business Plan"
> *whohastimeforthis.com*

Chapter 7

NDAS

Don't ask for an NDA — investors won't sign one. Your deck probably won't get in the hands of the competition, but you should assume it will. So don't share information that must remain confidential.

Can I get investors to sign an NDA?

Pros and cons to sending a deck

Your deck can get in the hands of the competition

When to send a deck

Do not submit any information or other materials that you consider to be confidential or proprietary. Because of the large number of business plans and related materials that we review, and the similarity of many such plans and materials, we cannot accept responsibility for protecting against misuse or disclosure of any confidential or proprietary information or other materials in the absence of our express written agreement to do so.

— SEQUOIA CAPITAL
Investors in Apple

Can I get investors to sign an NDA?

Getting an NDA from professional investors is almost impossible.
It can happen (like a rainbow!), but you shouldn't bother.

Investors don't sign NDAs because they don't want to get sued.
Competing companies tend to get started at the same time because
the market timing is right. Investors don't want to get sued if they
fund your competitor — so they don't sign NDAs.

You might think an NDA is a barrier to entry for your
competitors. Instead, it's just a barrier to getting funded. And it's
an insurmountable barrier: your request will be declined, or,
worse, you will be ignored because you haven't done your
homework. Don't spend so much time trying to build barriers to
entry that you're not even in the market yourself.

If you must keep something confidential, don't e-mail it to
investors and don't mention it in person. Keep your secrets secret.
Investors often look at a handful of similar companies at once.
Your plans probably won't get in the hands of the competition,
but you should assume they will.

Pros and cons to sending a deck

One of our blog readers e-mailed us with a question:

> "Do I really want my business plan floating out there in venture land? What if it gets to my competitors? Is it safe to send my deck to investors?"

First, focus on executing your plan so you can make it public instead of focusing on how to keep it private.

Second, sometimes we send decks, sometimes we don't. There is no right answer, but there are pros and cons that you can consider as you make your decision.

The pro to sending a deck is simple: it might help you get a meeting.

The first con: sending a deck can lower the effectiveness of your electronic pitch. Sometimes less is more. If you've got a great elevator pitch and introduction, do you need to send a relatively long document filled with arguments that are better delivered in person? The second con is...

Your deck can get in the hands of the competition

On skrenta.com, Rich Skrenta writes:

"So one day a few years ago I'm sitting in a VC's office having a chat. I had a few ideas rattling around in my head but the VC had his eyes on a then-current space which was hot. He tossed a business plan for one of the leading startups into my lap.

'Where'd you get this?' I asked.

'They gave it to me.'

He went on to talk about how he wanted to launch a company into the space as well, and I'd be a great VP Engineering. He said he knew a guy with some technology who could be CTO, had a VP Marketing in mind, and then we'd just need a world class CEO to round out the band.

I formed a theory that the process of seeking VC ended up calling your own competitors into existence. You'll meet with many more VCs than the 1-2 who end up funding you. But after seeing a company or two get funded in your space, the VCs who passed or weren't able to get in decide they want to have a bet in the space too. Fortunately they have the benefit of having heard your pitch and the opportunity to personally grill you at length on your approach."

Your deck probably won't get in the hands of the competition, but you should assume it will.

When to send a deck

Whether you send a deck depends on who wants the meeting most. Use this simple test:

> If you want the meeting more than they do, provide what they want. If they want a deck, give them a deck.

> If they want the meeting more than you do, provide what you want.

It all comes down to who has the most leverage — that's it. And leverage comes from traction. *Traction speaks louder than words.*

If you do send a deck, accept the fact that your elevator pitch and deck will contain information that you don't want printed on the front page of the *Wall Street Journal*. Accept the fact that no one currently cares enough about your company to put it there. And accept the fact that your ideas are worthless without execution.

Write, "Proprietary and Confidential. Please do not distribute. Prepared for Blue Shirt Capital," on the cover of your deck (some entrepreneurs write it on every page). Investors are less likely to forward your deck if their name is on it. If you're really worried, ask recipients, in writing, via e-mail, to kindly not distribute the deck outside their firm. A simple, "Please don't forward this outside your firm," will do.

If you don't want to send your full deck, consider sending a teaser deck: an abridged deck that has just enough information to get a meeting.

Remember to keep your secrets secret when you meet investors. An investor's handwritten notes can also get in the hands of the competition. And if an "evil" investor cares enough about your company to e-mail your deck to competitors, he will simply schedule a meeting with you and take notes.

Finally, you probably don't have many secrets. You might think you do — but you probably don't. Entrepreneurs tend to believe that there's a lot of value in their idea alone (there isn't) or their idea is particularly novel (it usually isn't). Work with an advisor who is experienced in your field to determine which of your secrets are really secrets.

When I see something that could be construed as competitive with a company in my portfolio, I generally mention this to the entrepreneur approaching me right away and give them control over whether or not they want to send me any other information... I know plenty of VCs that behave the way I do and plenty that don't.

— *Brad Feld, Managing Director, Foundry Group*
"Are Watermarks On Presentations
Useful?"
feld.com

You're going to have a hard enough time convincing your management team to work on the problem that you've decided to pursue, let alone having competitors go steal your idea and do the exact same thing.

— *Dharmesh Shah, Founder, HubSpot*
"Everything I Know About Startups"
onstartups.com

GROCKIT INTERVIEW

Brian Norgard, the founder of Newroo, interviews Farbood, the founder of Grockit. The topic: pitching Grockit.

Brian Norgard: Tell me about the funding process.

Farbood: I think raising money is great fun. The bottom line is that the money has to be spent. VCs are not in the business of holding their Limited Partner's investment in a 5% security. They have to spend the money on startups. So, either your startup gets the money or someone else's startup gets the money.

No VC has a perfect track record, nor do they pretend to. So, (1) either your idea or business sucks and the VCs knows it (despite their imperfect record, they are not bad at telling) or (2) you suck at explaining it. There is literally more money to invest than the world's VCs know what to do with.

Getting a meeting is another issue.

A referral is the single most powerful way to get into a VC firm. Most of their deals come from people they trust. If you can, go through this method, it works.

Yes. I think every founder fits in either situation 1 or 2.

Situation 1: Founder knows literally nobody in the VC community or, knows nobody who knows anybody. The founder is literally unconnected in anyway to anyone or anything in the VC or Angel world anywhere in the world.

Situation 2: Founder knows one, just one, or more people in, or connected to the VC/Angel world.

Response 1: I think the first situation is not realistic. Everybody knows somebody, who knows somebody. If you take yourself seriously as a internet founder, you're in LinkedIn and should be making sure you have a presence there. Make sure you follow and contribute to blogs like venturehacks.com and get people's blog reading lists so you know what blogs to follow. Get to know these people. Get yourself into situation 2. If you can't, you can't raise money, it's the first cutoff.

Response 2: Once you know one person, you ask them to connect you to another via an e-mail introduction. You ask the new person for a meeting. Keep adding quality people and impressing them with you and your business idea. Rinse and Repeat.

What did you learn from raising your Series A?

I learned that a disproportionately large percentage of VCs, relative to most populations I've encountered, are extremely smart, gregarious, easy to get along with, excited, positive and insightful. I'm usually surprised when I meet one that isn't.

This makes financings a far more positive experience than they would otherwise be and, just as importantly, makes the time and energy spent in meeting with them worthwhile in and of itself.

I also learned that, amazingly enough, of time, money and great people, time and great people are more scarce.

Any parting bits for entrepreneurs out there?

Make sure your pitch is great not good.

(From briannorgard.com)

PITCHING RESOURCES

Great blog posts on pitching we wish we had written.

·

1. Why startup pitches fail (and how to fix them) by Eric Ries

"Pitches usually fail because they answer the wrong questions. The right questions depend on the stage of your business—for example, some businesses are just getting started with an idea, while others are printing money. Focus your pitch on the key questions for your stage and if you keep getting non-key questions, something is wrong with your pitch. This post includes a hierarchy that you can use to classify your business and the key questions for each stage in the hierarchy."

Read the rest at *venturehacks.com/articles/why-pitches-fail*

2. Raising Money Using Customer Development by Steve Blank

"Notice that each of the 'Lessons Learned' slide has three major subheads and a graph: *Here's What We Thought. Here's What We Did. Here's What Happened. A Progress Graph.*

Here's What We Thought is you describing your initial set of hypotheses. *Here's What We Did* allows you to talk about building the first-pass of the products minimum feature set. *Here's What Happened* is the not so surprising story of why customers didn't react the way you thought they would. *A Progress Graph* on the right visually shows how far you've come (in whatever units of goodness you're tracking – revenue, units, users, etc.)"

Read the rest at *http://steveblank.com/2009/11/05/raising-money-with-customer-development*

3. How To Demo Your Startup by Jason Calacanis

"Talk about what you've done, not what you're going to do. Weak startups and their leaders seem to immediately start talk about "what's next," as opposed to focusing on the core product. Anyone can say we're going to add: a mobile version, collaborative filtering, an advertising network, visualizations, a marketplace, a browser plugin, a browser and a social network to their product. In fact, given the amount of open source and off the shelf software out there, combined with the large number of developers in the world, anyone can bolt these things on to their service in a week or three."

Read the rest at *http://www.techcrunch.com/2008/08/09/how-to-demo-your-startup*

STARTUP RESOURCES

VC and startup blogs that we read.

Venture Hacks

venturehacks.com
twitter.com/venturehacks

Must read

Fred Wilson – *A VC*
avc.com

Marc Andreessen
pmarca-archive.posterous.com

Paul Graham
paulgraham.com/articles.html

37signals
37signals.com/svn

Eric Ries – *Startup Lessons Learned*
startuplessonslearned.blogspot.com

More to read

Brad Feld and Jason Mendelson – *Ask the VC*
askthevc.com

Dharmesh Shah – *On startups*
onstartups.com

Josh Kopelman – *Redeye VC*
redeye.firstround.com

David Hornik – *VentureBlog*
ventureblog.com

Naval Ravikant – *StartupBoy*
startupboy.com

Should be posting more often

Bill Burnham – *Burnham's Beat*
tinyurl.com/4jb4mt

David Cowan – *Who Has Time For This?*
whohastimeforthis.com

Steve Barsh – *Barsh Bits*
blog.stevebarsh.com

Lawyers

Yoichiro "Yokum" Taku – *Startup Company Lawyer*
startupcompanylawyer.com

Up-and-comers

Mike Speiser – *Laserlike*
laserlike.com

Steve Blank
steveblank.com

Comedy

Venture Capital Wear
vcwear.com

ABOUT THE AUTHORS

You can reach both of us at team@venturehacks.com.

NIVI

I like helping entrepreneurs succeed —
like *Hamburger Helper for entrepreneurs.*

I've helped start companies like
Songbird, Grockit, and Kovio that have
been backed by firms including Sequoia,
Benchmark, and Kleiner Perkins.

I've also worked at venture capital firms
including Bessemer and Atlas Venture.

I have S.B., M.Eng., and "ABD" degrees from MIT in Electrical
Engineering and Computer Science, with a minor in Math. I was
also a National Science Foundation Graduate Research Fellow at
the MIT Media Lab.

I have two patents and have published a paper in *Science.* I used to
rock with *The Nitlings.* My personal blog is at nivi.com.

Naval Ravikant

I like to create improbable products that make money.

I've started a number of companies, including Epinions, Vast, Chainn, and Hive7. I'm an investor in Twitter, SocialMedia, Technorati, and other startups that you may yet hear about. I've been an advisor to XFire, Mercantila, and many others.

I studied Computer Science and Economics at Dartmouth. Now I study just about everything, with an emphasis on psychology, evolution, complex systems, human metabolism, and physics.

My personal blog is at startupboy.com.

THE END

Learn more at http://venturehacks.com.

Every startup has a chance to change the world, by bringing not just a new product, but an entirely new institution into existence.

— ERIC RIES
KPCB, Investors in Netscape

Made in the USA
Lexington, KY
15 March 2010